W.O.R.S.H.I.P.

VOLUME I

JOCELYN ANN BLOUNT

W.O.R.S.H.I.P. Volume I
By Jocelyn Blount

Printed in the United States of America

ISBN: 978-0-6152-0772-8

www.lulu.com
www.myspace.com/godsmanifestdestiny

Words

Of

Remembrance

Salvation

Healing

Inspiration

Purpose

Acknowledgements

To my Heavenly Father: Thanks a million☺. Thank you for inspiring me and gifting me to write each and every piece contained in this book; I truly count it a privilege and an honor.

To my Parents: Thanks for always supporting me. I could not have asked for greater parents!

To Zach and Clarisa Thomas: Thanks for being the two best mentors that ever were!

To Anisha Holden and Ashley Lipscomb: Thank you for being so supportive and helpful through this process!

Additional Thanks

My Family

Pastor Guns and my SCBC family

Min. Cullen and my SCA family

My Manna Fam

Beverly T. Gooden

This book is dedicated to all of you!

TABLE OF CONTENTS

Whispers to the Savior

"The prayer of a righteous man is
powerful and effective."

– James 5:16

(A Collection of Prayers)

Prayer of Desire

Now I lay me down to sleep;

I pray the Lord my soul to keep.

If I should die before I wake;

I pray the Lord my soul to take...

God, did I just give you permission to kill me?

No, I don't want die. I want you to heal me!

So please tonight don't take my soul;

Instead come in and make me whole.

Take away the guilt and the pain.

Erase these thoughts that are driving me insane-

Thoughts of low self esteem, depression, and fear.

God wipe away every single tear.

I don't want to be bound, I want to be free-

God break the shackles that are holding me.

I want to know You in a better way!

I want to hear Your voice all through the day!

I want to feel the power of Your love!

I want a peace that can only come from above!

I mean it this time; I want to live right!

This prayer is so different than the one I normally pray at night.

The tug on my heart I can no longer ignore;

It's like nothing I ever felt before.

I'm ready now to answer your call!

I'm blinded by Your light, just like Saul-

Ready to write to Your people, just like Paul.

You are the potter, I am the clay;

Lord I'm ready to do it Your way!

I've tried so hard to do it on my own-

Thought I was perfect, thought I was grown.

But that's not the life you called me to;

And this time around I'm living for you!

I present myself a living sacrifice.

I don't want to be evil, I want to be nice.

I no longer want to be depressed.

I ask to be released from the bondage of stress.

I know this is all a process that won't happen over night-

I just wanted You to know I've gotten back my sight.

I had been blinded by the sins of the world for so long;

Caught up in doing everything I knew was wrong.

But like I said before,

I've shut that door-

THAT AIN'T ME NO MORE!!!

You said in your word that any man be in Christ he is new;

And Lord that is all I'm asking of you!

A second chance to get things right;

And this time I won't put up a fight.

I'll do whatever you ask of me, Lord,

I'll read the Bible and share Your Word.

I'll change my circle of no good friends.

I'll even tell "o boy" we have to end.

...

I'm willing to do whatever it takes!

And I know I have a lot more sacrifices to make-

BUT, now my eyelids are heavy and I have to go

So...

Lord now slowly rock me to sleep;

And all these promises I promise to keep!

Prayer of Despair

Dear God,

I'm slipping and tripping, like I'm on a slippery slope.

I'm losing faith and losing hope.

I'm losing my ability to cope.

All I can do is sit around and mope-

And ask, when did things start to go bad?

And what happened to the joy and peace I once had?

Why can't I no longer make magic with a pen and a pad?

And, why after all you've done for me, am I still sad?

Why do I find it easier to wear a frown?

God I feel like I'm letting you down;

Like I'm hurting you-

And all I want is to please you in all I do...

Well, I know you're listening and I know you care;

So please hear this prayer: my prayer of despair.

My Child,

Quit it!

You're not letting me down a bit.

You are putting up a strong fight;

I heard your cries and prayers last night.

But you're not trusting in me with all your might,

And of my bigger plan, you're losing sight.

15

So just allow me to shed some light...

I already told you to let go and let Me,

But you're not taking my advice, I see.

You're not allowing my perfect will to be;

And that's what's really hurting me.

You told me your heart and soul said yes,

And no matter what I asked, you would try your best.

But you forgot the Prayer of Desire, I guess;

Because you are dealing with unnecessary stress.

I guess you don't think I can handle your mess.

Or maybe you just have no time to cast on me all your cares.

You are slowly deleting me from your schedule; Are you aware?

Have you seen the decrease in the time you set aside to pray?

Have you been listening to what I have to say?

Have you picked up your bible this week to read?

Do you continue to perform your daily good deed?

Or have you become too busy to live for me?

*Now that I've elevated you, have you forgotten the One who gave you
life?*

The One who took away all your pain and strife?

The One who made your life brand new?

The One who gifted you to do what you do?

The One who's grace and mercy has kept you?

The One who opened your eyes and altered your view? ...

My child stop crying, it's okay,

Tomorrow is a brand new day,

You have another chance to get things right.

But for now, get some rest, and have a good night.

But how can I get a good night's sleep?

All I can do is lay here and weep.

How could I been so careless with my time?

Wasting it, like it was mine-

Like it wasn't given to me to bring glory to You.

So tomorrow I know what I have to do-

I have to get my priorities straight.

I have to realize what deserves my time and what can wait!

I HOPE TO ALL WHO READ THIS YOU WERE BLESSED AND NOT ONLY THAT BUT CHALLENGED AS WELL. MANY TIMES WE UNINTENTIONALLY DEVOTE OUR TIME, TALENT, AND MONEY TO THINGS THAT ARE NOT IN LINE WITH OUR DESTINY. THAT IS NOT TO SAY THESE THINGS ARE BAD, THEY ARE JUST NOT A PART OF THE LIFE GOD HAS CALLED US TO. I AM CONVINCED IF MORE PEOPLE WOULD FULLY OPERATE IN THE GIFTS GOD GAVE THEM AND STOPPED TRYING TO SPREAD THEMSELVES THIN OR DO ANOTHER'S JOB, THEN MORE KINGDOM WORK COULD BE ACCOMPLISHED; AND IN THE END THAT SHOULD BE EVERYONE'S MAIN GOAL (TO DO EVERYTHING TO THE

GLORY OF GOD AND THE UPLIFTING OF HIS KINGDOM). SO WITH THAT SAID, IF YOU KNOW WHAT YOUR DESTINY IS, DEVOTE YOUR TIME TO WALKING IN IT AND FUFILLING IT. AND IF YOU DON'T KNOW, OR ONLY KNOW THE HALF, DEVOTE YOUR TIME TO FINDING OUR WHAT PART GOD WANTS YOU TO PLAY IN THE CHRISTIAN BODY, THEN GIVE IT YOUR ALL!!![1]

---

[1] Scripture of Reference (1 Corinthians 12:17-20)

Prayer of Repentance

Daddy, tonight I come to You with a heavy heart;

I have so much to say, I don't know where to start.

I've stepped out of Your Will; I've disobeyed Your Word,

And for all that I've done I'm sorry Lord.

I've allowed my flesh and feelings to take control-

So tonight I cry out to You with a hurting soul.

I've allowed my sins and hurt to pile up inside.

I'm no longer being led by my spirit, but by my ego and pride.

I no longer acknowledge You in all my ways...

To be honest, we haven't talked in days.

Instead I've been carrying around all my burdens with me;

Which is not the way You intended it to be.

You want me to cast all my cares on You,

And seek Your Will in all I do.

So, Daddy, tonight I beg You to forgive.

Teach me Your ways. Teach me how to live.

Wash away all the sin and the dirt.

Heal all anger, depression, and hurt.

Lift the heavy burden weighing me down.

Give me the power to tear down strongholds keeping me bound.

Give me the wisdom to know the devil's trap.

Give me patience during this process, so I won't snap.

Give me courage to continue to stand as a bold witness.

Teach me love, trust, and most importantly, forgiveness,

Because God I want to turn away from my past.

I want this choice and change to last.

I no longer want to fall victim to the same sin,

Because You have given me victory over it. I must win.

No longer will I succumb to this reprobate mind,

But Your love and forgiveness, at last, I will find.

And just before I close out this prayer of repentance,

I want to Thank You for being a God of a second chance!

I love You and I bless Your holy name.

Thank You for Your faithfulness; every day the same.

Thank You for always being a listening ear,

And Thank You for being a friend so dear.

Amen

Not My Will

But Thy Will Be Done

"Yet not what I will, but what you will."
- Mark 14:36

Get It Together

I've finally learned to completely trust You
And believe You have a purpose for all You do.
I finally believe all things are working for my good
And not everything is meant to be understood;
Because You already know the plans for me.
Not plans to harm me but plans for prosperity.
You didn't need me when You made the earth,
Or when You gave mankind birth,
Or when You made creatures big and small.
No, You didn't need my help at all.
So why do I think You need me now?
You've been running things forever- You know how!
So I'm going to stop and let You take the lead.
You created me- You know what I need.
You know my thoughts and actions before they exist.
Wow! I could just continue down the list.
But I won't, because you already know. I'll just say...
I surrender Daddy, You can have Your way!

It is time to let go and let God do His thing. You do not belong to

yourself; you belong to our heavenly Father. He created you for

Himself. You are what He is using to bring glory to His name. Let us stop getting it twisted; God is not to be what you use to bring glory to your name. If it was not for Him, you would not have a name, you would not even be here. So think about that the next time you think you can make it without God, or next time you think you did something on your own. God is the giver and sustainer of life... YOU CAN NOT LIVE WITHOUT HIM, LITERALLY!!! There is no way you can live without God and if you could, what quality of life would that be!?! At the same time your quality of life also suffers when you decide to put restrictions and limits on God's reign in your life. This is the same God who created the universe... imagine how big that is... you can't can you? Now imagine a God who is bigger! Do you really think you can pack Him in a box and carry Him around with you when it is convenient? God, being your creator, do you think you can only give Him access to certain parts of His creation? LET'S GET REAL!!! God wants ALL of you, ALL of the time. And I just believe that in these last and evil days God is looking for people that are aware that age, color, nationality, denomination, past history, education, clothes, background, circumstances, mistakes, etc. DON'T MATTER. I am convinced He is looking for the people that are SINCERELY SEEKING Him, people that are TRUSTING in Him with their total being, people who ARE NOT ASHAMED of their faith no matter what the situation. God is looking for the radical bold Christians that know YEA THOUGH I WALK THROUGH THE VALLEY OF THE SHADOW OF DEATH, I WILL FEAR NO EVIL! Yes I believe He is looking for the truly sold out saints that are crazy enough to believe every word He ever said and every promise He ever made. God is truly tired of part time saints and so am I! It is time out for the fake and phony. Time is truly running out... STOP STRADDLING THE FENCE!!! When asked whether you want to go to heaven or hell, the answer is so easy. So why is it not that easy to pick up the bible, or to pray, or to witness! People want the title and benefits of being a Christian but do not want to do the work of one! It is time out for trying to get the best of both worlds... CHOOSE YE THIS DAY WHOM YE SHALL SERVE!!! And serve Him wholeheartedly, like your life depends on it... because when it really boils down, it does!

GOD USES ORDINARY PEOPLE TO DO EXTRAORDINARY THINGS

This piece was inspired by the theme to a Vacation Bible School I attended when I was younger. I will never forget the words to the theme song: "God uses ordinary people to do extraordinary things". We sang that every night right before we learned about another biblical character who had humble beginnings, an insignificant past, a dull life, or who lacked in areas, but God still used them to do an awesome and mighty work. I was reminded of this as I read the book of Luke... wow I must say Jesus had some of the most humble beginnings I have ever heard of. Who would have imagined little baby Jesus born in a manger to a carpenter would be the Savior of the World; obviously not the people who watched him grow up and knew his humble beginnings (Mark 6:1-6). That very thing is so common, especially today; it is the people that you grew up with that know where you come from and what you have been through that doubt God's move in your life the most. That is why I can tell someone that I went to middle school with, what is going on in my life right now and they will laugh and call me a liar. That is why your family looks at you strange sometimes and your friends just ain't feeling you right now. But we as believers have to stop limiting God and who He can use. I personally believe God can use any and everyone He created. He is not just limited to the people who grew up in the church, or the prestigious, or the intelligent, or the person voted "Most Likely to Succeed", or the person who comes from a family of holy people. No, HE IS WILLING AND ABLE TO USE ANYONE WILLING AND ABLE TO BE USED! You do not have to have any prerequisites or enormous amounts of anything. You just have to surrender to God the little you do have and leave it up to Him to multiply it. In Mark 6:30-44, He took two fish and five loaves of bread and fed 5,000+ people. Wow that has me excited; knowing I serve a God who gives increase like that and who will use ordinary me to do extraordinary things!

I Surrender All

God I come humbly bowing at your feet;

I don't know what else to do.

So with tear stained eyes and up-raised arms,

I surrender my all to YOU! ...

"All to Jesus I surrender".

It's more than just a song.

It's the only thing I could do,

When my life was going wrong.

But now I'm beginning to realize

That it is not enough;

To just give God control of me

When things are going rough.

God should not only be my problem solver,

Or the giver of all my gifts.

NO, that is a mistaken philosophy,

My mindset had to shift.

God should not just be called on when things are going bad;

Nor should he be used as Kleenex when life makes me sad.

God should not just be the One to put a smile upon my face,

But the One who holds my hand, no matter what the case.

And to me that seems so obvious,

And to me that seems so fair.

He gave me this life to live,

So the least I can do is share.

He already knows my outcome;

He created me with a blueprint and plan.

And all I have to do for that to be fulfilled

Is put my life COMPLETELY in His hand.

God wants every part of me;

My mind, body, and soul.

He doesn't want any piece of me broken;

He wants me to be whole.

And now that I better understand His purpose and wants for me;

And now a clearer vision, I'm able to see...

A better person I'm desiring to be!!!

But I know I can't do it on my own,

No matter how much I've developed and how much I've grown;

Because I was not created to walk through this life alone.

I was created to always haste unto His throne.

And to His throne I'll always haste,

Because living this life without Him is a big waste.

Not giving God COMPLETE control,

Was like living with a big black hole-

Somewhere where there was supposed to be a heart and a soul;

No longer could I be a creation, not being operated by my Creator.

After all, who else knows what I was put here for.

So after being miserable for so long,

And after seeing my way of living as wrong.

I heard the lyrics to the song-

And through that I've been made strong.

So no longer do I have to wait until night to pray,

Because I talk with my Daddy all through the day.

No longer do I have to worry if I'm pleasing in His sight,

Because He walks with me, and corrects me if I ain't right.

No longer do I have to worry about things in life,

Because I give it all to God and he diminishes my strife.

No longer do I have to live with regret, guilt, and shame...

I've been REEDEEMED; He's cleared my name.

NO LONGER DO I HAVE TO LIVE WITH REGRET, GUILT,

AND SHAME....

I'VE BEEN REDEEMED; HE'S CLEARED MY NAME.

(Sorry you all that repeat was for me, but sometimes you have to

look in the mirror and talk to what you see)

No longer do I have to be confused about the moves I make.

I'm willing to sell out; and I'm doing it all for my God's sake.

But none of this would have ever been, if that one thing I didn't

do; and that was lift my hands and raise my voice and say,

"God I surrender my ALL to YOU!!!!"

I'll Trust You

Though You slay me,
And bring me to my knees.
Yet will I trust You
To do whatever You please.

Because You know the plans,
The plans You have for me.
And You know my end;
You know what You've destined me to be.

So who am I to question?
So who am I to doubt?
Who am I to not believe?
Who am I to scream and shout?

For You said to have faith,
Faith the size of a mustard seed.
And to put all my trust in You;
Trust You wherever You lead.

So God that's what I intend to do,
Even when I can't see the good.
I'll follow Your ordered path,

Even when reasons aren't understood.

Because I know You love me,
And have my best interest at hand.
I know all things are working together,
Although those things I may not understand.

But even more than that,
I know that everything is a test.
And it's only upon completion…
That I will come out my very BEST!

Is Your All on the Altar?

Pain... lost... broken again.
Streams of tears that never end;
Because I knew what was right,
    but I chose sin.
This pain I feel lies so deep within.

I feel it every time I think of the act.
I didn't know it would have such a
    great impact.
How was I supposed to know this
    was how I would react?
I feel like the scum of the universe
    to be exact.

But as I sit here and cry and grieve;
I'm reminded of what and in whom I
    believe!
His forgiving love, I need to receive.
The heavy pain and burden, He can
    relieve.

So on my knees I bow to pray.
And as I begin to tell Daddy about

my day,
All feelings of guilt and shame go away.
No more feelings of dismay!

I continue to engage in this conversation.
I tell God all of my hurt and frustration.
Then I ask for forgiveness and reconciliation,
And for the strength to fight future temptation.

I continue to pray then tears come to my eyes,
As things become plain and I start to realize...

Everything I told God, He already knew.
His response to me was "I was just waiting
    on you!"
And "You know this talk is long overdue".
"By the way tell the rest of my people I'm
    waiting on some of them too."

So now my question is: Have you given God your all?
Time is running out, there is no time to stall!
He is on the mainline, just give Him a call!
He's on standby, waiting to pick you up when you fall!

Let Go and Let God

God, yes I know;

I hear you whispering in my ear to let it go.

Why are you holding on to the fear and the pain?

You know you don't want to go through this all over again.

Child, you need to relax, you're under too much stress.

You need to start giving stuff to me and letting me do the rest.

I know you like to be in control; but I am more than able,

And I guarantee you'll feel better and be more stable.

I promise if you'll just put your trust in Me,

And walk in My will and allow it to be-

Then you will see that I'm working things for your good.

What's funny is I thought you understood!

But I can see the doubt in your eyes-

Hear the fear at night in your cries.

I know you don't think everything I told you was lies;

But you're trying too hard to analyze.

Don't worry about how I'm going to work things out;

Just trust in Me and have no doubt.

Have the faith the size of a mustard seed.

Give up your agenda and let Me take the lead.

Stop fighting my plan,

And just give me your hand.

Now, My child, do you understand? ...

Even when you don't know what the end results going to be-

Even when the victory you can't see,

You have to learn to let go and let Me!

Lord I'm Available to You!

I was watching the Lott Carey Montage 07 from the Lott Carey Foreign Baptist Mission youth seminar and the song "Lord I'm Available to You", was playing in the background. I could not help but cry, as I saw picture after picture and thinking of just how much the LC family was a blessing to the people of Raleigh and the surrounding cities that week. There was gleaning, the Children's Home, Polk Detention Center, Habitat for Humanity, Helping Hands, the soup kitchen, Salvation Army, and others. Wow, because a few hundred people made themselves available, a few thousand were blessed... THAT'S AMAZING! I then began to think about the mission teams at my church; one just coming back from Trinidad, one still in Kenya... touching people that may have never been touched if it was not for them making themselves available. Now of course I understand, not everyone has the opportunity to go on a mission trip and not many people go on a mission trip everyday of their lives. But everyday you have the opportunity to reach out to and spread the Gospel to others. This is our duty as Christians as stated in Matthew 28:19-20. (We all have different gifts and callings but this is our ultimate goal). Everyday, each of us is presented with opportunities to help people, to encourage people, and to be a blessing to people. Colossians 4:5 says "Be wise in the way you act toward outsiders, make the most of every opportunity. Let your conversation be always full of grace, seasoned with salt, so that you may know how to answer everyone." It could be something as small as smiling at someone who is frowning, giving a friend in need a ride, holding the door open for someone, or giving someone money to buy something to eat. 1 John 3:16- 17 says "This is how we know what love is: Christ laid down his life for us. And we ought to lay down our lives for our brothers. If anyone has material possessions and sees his brother in need but has no pity on him, how can the love of God be in him?" There are so many people in this world hurting and lacking in every aspect of their life. But we have found the ANSWER, and it is our job to share it. I use to be skeptical when people would say "you are the only bible some people may read" or "the only Jesus some people may see"; but o how true that is, and if you always seem to have an attitude, and drama, or always upset or if you are unapproachable and put up a barrier, you could be greatly hindering your witness. But reach out to others as Christ has reached out to you (Philippians 3:12). In dealing with others always exhibit the fruits of the Spirit, "love, joy, peace, patience, kindness, goodness, faithfulness, gentleness and self-control" (Galatians 5:22-23). It is when you begin to produce that kind of healthy, ripe fruit that others can partake of it and be blessed. But the greatest way to be a blessing to others is to make yourself available to be used. So many times we get caught up in our schedule and our wants, desires and the busyness we create for ourselves. So many times we wake up and tell God our schedule for the day. But how much more fulfilling would your day be if you woke up and asked God what He wanted you to do, what he wanted you to wear, where he wanted you to go, what he wanted you to say? How awesome, if you woke up every morning and presented your body a living

41

sacrifice to God (Romans 12:1)... If every morning, before you even got out of bed you connected with God... Wow, how glorious that would be, to truly be in the will of God. How wonderful, if like the song says, we gave back the tools He has given us, if we let God have free reign over our eyes, our ears, our hands, our voice, and our gifts both natural and spiritual. I just sit here and imagine how much God delights in us when we surrender and open ourselves to be used by Him. And who doesn't want God to delight in them? So empty yourself, die to yourself and your will and become available to be used by God!

"Use me Lord to show someone the way and enable me to say, "My storage is empty and I am available to you"

In His Favor
(Life in God)

"For you died, and your life is now hidden with Christ in God."

- Colossians 3:3

Contentment

I may not be the most beautiful person in the world.

But God created me fearfully and wonderfully…

So I am content!

I may not be the smartest person in the world.

But God has granted me wisdom…

So I am content!

I may not be the most confident person in the world.

But I can do all things through Christ who strengthens me…

So I am content!

I may not be the richest person in the world.

But God has made me prosperous…

So I am content!

I may not be the most loved person in the world.

But God's unconditional love has consumed me…

So I am content!

I may not be the most recognized person in the world.

But my reward is waiting in heaven…

So I am content!

I may not be the most appreciated person in the world.

But I've learned to encourage myself...

So I am content!

I may not be the healthiest person in the world.

But God still wakes me up every morning...

So I am content!

I may not have all my wants.

But God has supplied all my needs...

So I am content!

I may not be all I want to be.

But thank God I'm not what I use to be...

So I am content![2]

In a world where depression, low self esteem, envy, jealousy, coveting, disappointment, and emptiness is running rapid, I have found contentment in God.

---

[2] This poem was inspired by the song "Contentment" by The Anointed Pace Sisters as well as Philippians 4:11-13

Don't Mess with My Peter or My Judas!

Many people struggle with friends. Some have friends betray them. Some have friends doubt them. But many just misunderstand the role of their friends. Whatever the case may be, I am a true believer that everything we face now Jesus did as well. He too had people in his company that may not have been the easiest to deal with and down right defiant at times. But Jesus knew the necessity of Peter and Judas. And it is through his encounters with these two gentlemen that we see a lot of Jesus' character and we learn how we should deal with people like this in our lives.

(Matthew 16:21-26)

Let us start with Peter. He has to be my favorite disciple, mainly because he was the realest in my opinion. Many of us can relate to him because he was practical. He was the one who always said what everyone else was thinking or feeling. He honestly expressed his doubts and fears to Jesus; not to be rude but to show his concern. He told Jesus how he felt about things, even when Jesus didn't ask him... I am sure all of us have been Peter before and I am sure we all have friends who are Peters. The friend that is not always quick to jump on what you are doing. The one not always focused on the best solution but the easiest one. The friend that is not always in tune with you and your goals and purpose. Yes, we all have our Peters. But Jesus does not get mad with Peter, he does not stop being around him; but He is firm with him. He never let Peter's lack of faith affect how He felt and thought, but He often used it as an opportunity to minister to others, as seen in the above passage and Matthew 14: 25-33. Many times in our lives, it is our Peters that keep us seeking God for confirmation. It is our Peters that help us stand firm in our faith. Our Peters even keep us constantly reminding ourselves of our purpose and calling. So when your Peters begin to work your nerves or seem overly negative and doubtful, just know they are doing their job... Now you do yours.

(Matthew 26: 47- 51)

Next, we have Judas. Judas in many people's minds is the most hated disciple. On the contrary, he is among my favorites. Yes, he betrayed Jesus but that betrayal led to the salvation of mankind. Yes, he traded loyalty for money, but that only pushed Jesus further into His destiny. Jesus' knowledge of his betrayal brought Him to his knees. You know, it is not the people who treat you right and are nothing but nice to you that bring you close to God; but it is the people you know are phony, and backstabbers, and mean, that keep you constantly before God. It is like people say: "Many of you wouldn't pray if it wasn't for trials and storms". Some people push you to the point where all you can do is pray. But as we see in the scriptures, Jesus never had an attitude with Judas, He never treated him differently, and He did not even call him out until the very end. Jesus let Judas betray Him, and He did not try to stop him, because He knew the significant role Judas played in the Will of God. Jesus knew that battle was not even for Him to fight. So now when the Judas arises in your life and begins to act phony and back bite you, just know they are doing their job... So just watch them push you closer to God and closer to your destiny.

No matter what, never let your encounters with others discourage your relationship or faith in God and what He is speaking to you. Many times people we encounter, even our friends, are jealous, angry, hurting, confused, disturbed and they may take it out on us, when we are not even the source of their pain. This often causes us to want to retaliate; but Ephesians 6:12 tells us that "we wrestle not against flesh and blood, but against principalities, against powers, against the rulers of the darkness of this world, against spiritual wickedness in high places." So if it is anyone we should get angry with, it is the devil! But we are so busy being mad at flesh and blood, when we need to be casting out the evil spirits that have taken residence in the flesh... but that is another topic.

Endless Possibilities

I'll say it now, as I've said it before:

Only God knows what He has in store.

Ears can not hear, nor eyes see,

All of what He has planned for me.

And to me that is exciting to know;

It causes my anticipation to grow.

Just to think the creator of all things,

The Lord of Lords and King of Kings

Specifically planned out my destiny.

He made me who He wanted me to be.

He placed in me each gift and trait.

He preordained and destined my fate.

I was fearfully and wonderfully made.

And now with all that said...

I know my possibilities have no end;

Where I'm going is bigger than where I've been.

I know there is no limits, not even the sky.

My visions and dreams are what I live by.

I refuse to be put in a box by man;

For someone more powerful has my life in His hand.

So to all the nay sayers, you have been blocked out.

My life has no room for fear and doubt.

Besides, once you stop limiting what God's trying to do,

You'll see He has endless possibilities in store for you too!

Misery for Ministry

When we first get saved many are under the impression that everything will be peaches and cream. Many are under the impression that because they are a Christian everything will be easy and no more hassles; and many times they are correct if they are just happy with the gift of salvation. But for us Christians that are not just satisfied with a "get into heaven free pass", for us Christians not just satisfied with a mediocre life, for us Christians looking to obtain all God has predestined for our lives, for us Christians not ashamed to spread the gospel of Jesus Christ any and everywhere, for us Christians sold out for Christ; for God I live, for God I die... Yes, for us Christians, everything is not always going to be easy. There are going to be some battles we have to face, some obstacles we have to overcome, some tears we have to cry, some pain we have to endure, some pride we have to swallow, some set backs we have to get over, some situations that are going to be uncomfortable, some friends we are going to lose, some changes that are going to leave us lost and confused... Yes there will be some people that will talk about you, yes there will be some sleepless nights, some pain, some suffering, some wrestling with God, some questioning God, some pressure … But I am convinced, as Paul was in Romans 8:17-18, that because I am God's heir, my present sufferings are not worth comparing with the glory that will be revealed in me. I'm just crazy enough to believe, just the way a mother forgets her labor pains when she sees her baby's face, that the day I see my Savior's face the pain I had to endure on earth will not mean anything. I am just radical enough to believe that anything God brings me to, he will bring me through. I just trust God enough to believe He won't put more on me than I can bear. I know enough science to know that you have to put gold in the middle of the fire to get rid of all its impurities; and having lived an imperfect life for 18 years, I've learned that it was my mistakes, my shortcomings, my pain, my heartaches, and my brokenness that molded me into the person I am today. And through all of this I have come to the conclusion that sometimes one must go through misery for their ministry.

Going through misery for my ministry... It is a phrase I first heard watching Karen Clark Sheard on a TBN broadcast. She was sharing her testimony about how she had been sick and she said some stuff that really inspired me... and I quote, "Don't be looking at all this, what's going on, and glamour. People don't know you have to pay a price to get to the next level and to have His precious anointing. But I promised God, if that's what I had to go through- if it had to take me going through misery for my ministry; That's alright, I'm willing and able. You can send me Jesus I'll go for You, I'll walk for You, whatever it takes God, cause I belong to You." And as I sat there and kept listening to her saying this in my head, I thought to myself, wow that makes a lot of sense. I mean just think about how much more effective your witness is after you have been through the trial. "By His stripes you are healed" is a lot more powerful coming out of the mouth of someone who has been sick and has experienced God's healing power first hand. Telling someone about the joy God gives is more meaningful from someone who has been so depressed they have contemplated suicide. Stories of God's delivering power are more credible coming from the mouth of a former addict or someone who has been bound. Jesus' redeeming power means so much more coming from the mouth of someone who remembers what it was like not to have salvation and someone who knows they have not been perfect all of their life. So I was convinced, after hearing Karen's testimony and hearing her inspiring words, that I could make this same promise to God. And it seemed the second I spoke it out my mouth, the ride started. Things began to get harder, but I remembered the promise I had made to God and more importantly the promises He had made to me. I remembered my life was in His hands and I was following His lead. I remembered that as long as I was in His will and in His presence I was in the safest place in the whole wide world…so the temporary inconveniences (for permanent improvements) were nothing for me to fear. God did not send these problems in my life to kill me or to discourage me. On the contrary, He sent them to make me strong; because what does not kill you ultimately makes you stronger. In my weakness, God's strength is made evident through me; which is the reason I did not ask God to remove these problems from my life, just as He did not remove the thorn from Paul's flesh.

Not only was I able to find strength while going through "misery for my ministry" from God's promises made personally to me and His promises made in the bible; I was also able to be encouraged by others who had to go through misery for their ministry. Noah had to go through the ark, Moses had to go through the wilderness, The Three Hebrew boys had to go through the fiery furnace, David had to go through Goliath and Saul, Daniel had to go through the lion's den, Joseph had to go through his brothers, Paul and Silas had to go through prison. This just names a few people in the bible and a few periods of misery they had to go through for their ministry. And while each and every one of their stories is very encouraging and insightful to going through and of God's sustaining power while you are on the battlefield for Him;

fhere is still one person who tops them all when it comes to going through "misery for your ministry" and that is my Lord and Savior Jesus Christ. We see in Mark 14:32-36 how Jesus dreaded being crucified, because even though He was God, he was still flesh and his humanness displayed sorrow and distress, to the point where he asked if there was any way possible that He did not have to go through with it. But Jesus did not stop there, after venting to God, He let Him know that even though that was how he felt, this thing was not about Him. It was about God's will being done... How many of us say that? How many of us recognize it is never about how we feel or what we think should be... it is strictly about God's will being done and glory being brought to His name. We were created to praise and glorify God. He sent Jesus to save us so we may have a life to the fullest and in that life we are to tell others of salvation. Those are our purposes and our goals ... anything else is extra. I've learned that life is not about what I want; honestly I do not know what I want. I may think I do, but only the One who created me really knows. You can not get the fullest potential out of an invention unless you go to the original inventor. You may think you know its total purpose and design; but you may miss something. And in this life I do not want to miss anything; I want all God has for me. I want everything God has birthed in me to come into fruition. I want to utilize every gift; I want nothing to be wasted. That includes my time; because after all, only what you do for Christ will last. So with all that said ... I do not mind going through misery for my ministry. I do not mind having to go through something for someone else will not have to someday. I do not mind laboring for God, because you truly reap what you sow. I do not mind sharing with Christ in His sufferings, because I will also share with Him in His glory.

Jesus was God's son and he was mocked, spit on, humiliated, stabbed, and nailed to a cross, hung to die.... Are we any better than him? And are we not called God's children as well? So are we exempt from suffering? If Jesus Christ a perfect man endured hardships, what makes us think that we won't? The question is: Are you prepared to do whatever it takes for your ministry and to bring glory to His name?

Provision for Your Vision

Let us first start by talking about vision itself... People must have vision or they will perish (Proverbs 29:18)... point blank. If you do not see anything past your "right now" situation, when your "right now" situation is not great you will lose your will to live and persevere. It is like being a runner not knowing where the finish line is or not even knowing there is a finish line, because you have never seen it. So you run around aimlessly, exhausted and frustrated, not knowing in which direction to go... This is no way to live! Yes, you are still running. Yes, you are still using your ability. Yes, you are still getting distance, but how effective are you if you never reach your goal, achieve your full potential, or become all God has destined for you (1 Corinthians 9:24-27)? But how can you be focused and pressed towards a mark you can not see? That is why I have so much respect for visionaries, dreamers, and prophets; and I'm crazy enough to believe we all possess those abilities to an extent. So why are so many people not walking in their destiny? Why are so many visions not being fulfilled? Why are so many dreams never lived? I believe it is because of the devil's lies. That voice that tells you that "you are not good enough to do that", "that will never work", "who told you that you could do that"... But it is time to tell the devil, "when God tells me something, I believe it and that settles it." I serve a God that specializes in the impossible. There is also this other lie that has discouraged people since the beginning of time... and that is "you don't have the resources to do that", "you don't have the necessary material", "you only have such and such amount". But we have to be like Abraham and know that God is Jehovah Jireh! He will provide. When God tells you to do something or shows you doing something, He does not ask you do you have the necessary qualifications or equipment, or if you think it is feasible. See what many believers do not understand is GOD DOESN'T NEED YOUR PERMISSION; HE JUST WANTS YOUR CONSENT! MY GOD! HE DOESN'T NEED YOU TO TELL HIM WHAT TO DO IN YOUR LIFE OR HOW TO DO IT; HE JUST WANTS YOU TO LET HIM DO IT!!! HE WANTS A YES TO HIS WILL AND HIS

WAY. HE WANTS YOU TO SAY YES TO THE DESTINY HAS ALREADY PLANNED FOR YOU! Therefore He already knows what you need before you speak it! Just look to heaven and receive what you need. This brings me to one of my favorite bible stories; when Jesus fed the 5,000+ people with two fish and five loaves of bread. I believe the moment Jesus told his disciples to feed the people, he already saw them fed. He then took the little He had and gave thanks, blessed it and raised it to heaven and after that, the little it appeared He had fed 5,000+. But the part of the story most people forget, but which is the best part; after everyone had eaten and became satisfied, the disciples picked up quite a few baskets of leftovers. Just like God, always showing off. He will not only provide you with what you need right then but He will give you overflow for the next time! That is how the Father works... Jehovah Jireh... MORE THAN ENOUGH! So next time you sit and think you do not have what you need to fulfill the will of God... look to heaven and praise the God of Provision and Overflow!!!

Simply Put- Salvation Made Easy

I wanted to write on this subject ever since I heard the Fred Hammond song "Simply Put". The song basically talks about how a lot of times we overcomplicate spirituality and get hung up on religion but the bottom line is God loves us and we belong to Him, and sometimes that is all you need to know to make it through.

When the day is over and you find yourself all alone in your bed, when the music fades out, when the choir sits down, when the preacher says his last amen, when the fellowship ends, when the meeting is over, when the mission team comes back home, when the service is complete... After the prophecies have been spoken, after the tongues have been interpreted, after the communion has been taken, after the hands have been laid, after the scriptures have been quoted, the clichés recited, the benediction given... When it is just you and nobody or nothing else but God... At that very moment denominations, church politics, meetings, organizations, philosophies, theology, doctrine... they just don't mean as much. At that moment, all that matters is that God loves me and He loves me soooo much that He sent His Son to suffer and die, so that I could have an abundant and everlasting life. Those other things are great, but if it was not for God's love, none of those things would matter or even exist. I think Hezekiah Walker said it best when he said, "When the song is over, when the music stops, do you know Jesus? Does He live in your heart?" And simply put, that is what everything boils down to. Salvation does not have to be complicated or difficult, it is free and available to anyone who believes and receives God's love through the sacrifice of His son. And when you really begin to embrace God's love and the gift of salvation it becomes so much easier to share it effectively and genuinely with others; which is our number one duty as Christians. So just remember when things get complicated and you lose sight, simply put God loves you and because of that everything else will ultimately work itself out. Find comfort and strength in that and Remember- Keep it simple!!!

True Worshippers Are an Endangered Species

God is not superficial, by a far shot. He is so deep and so infinite; and it makes our petty mess and thoughts look so shallow. But so many people think that God is caught up on the things we are caught up on, but I am here to tell you God ain't on the yearbook staff, the gossip circle, or at "the meeting after the meeting". He isn't looking for best dressed; He is looking for the person who is wearing a dress they bought last season in order to be able to sow into ministry. He isn't looking for most gifted and talented; He is looking for the person using the gifts and talents He gave them, to bring glory to His name. He isn't looking for the person wearing a cross around their neck, but the person bearing the cross of Jesus on their back. He isn't looking for a person wearing white from head to toe; He is looking for the person pure and holy on the inside. He isn't concerned with what choir sings; He cares that they know Jesus in their heart. He isn't concerned with what song they are singing; He cares that they are singing from their hearts as a form of praise and worship to Him. He isn't even concerned with what they have on... He just wants what they are saying to be heard. He isn't looking for the usher board with the sharpest uniform; He is looking for people who can usher His presence in. My God! He isn't looking for a saint who can recite the covenant from memory; but more like the one who can recite His Word from memory because they have written it in their heart. He isn't looking for a person who can give the most to the church; He is looking for the radical tither who can barely pay their bills, but trust God enough to give Him their last dime. He isn't looking for a person who can pray the longest and use the most clichés; He is looking for the person who prays from a pure and honest heart. He isn't looking for a person who knows how to "play church"; but He is looking for the person yearning to be in His presence, to enter the holy of holies, to worship in spirit and truth, the person desiring to rest in His secret place, people trying to go beyond the veil. But we are so caught on what someone looks like on the outside or what they appear to be, that we no longer look at people's spirit and true character. Someone who may seem to have it going on may be the person who needs the most encouragement. Just like someone who looks like they are struggling may have more faith than you can ever imagine. But many times we judge people before they have a chance to show who they really are. Two women walk in church; one with a white suit, the other with tattered baggy jeans and an oversized t-shirt... who do you think is more holy?... Come on people... Are we really that shallow? That stuff does not faze God. He is not concerned with flesh; He isn't concerned with your lip service. God is concentrating on what is on the inside, because the bible says your body is the temple of God. So make sure your heart is pleasing to the Lord; as well as make sure your worship is true.

When God Gives You a Sneak Preview

As many of us think about our past and even the present state we find ourselves in, we see times of spiritual and mental immaturity. We see times of uncertainty and confusion. We see times of doubt and mistakes. We see times of unfulfilled dreams, untouched potential, and incomprehensible vision. But there will be a time when your dreams will be fulfilled, your potential will be maximized, and your visions understood. This time, my friends, is the future.

I know many of you want to ask me "how can I speak on the future?" A time I have not traveled to; a place I have not been. How can I speak on the future when many have heard for years "No one knows what the future holds". Well I beg to differ; there is someone who knows all about the future, matter of fact He holds tomorrow. He is my Father and best friend; and because of this fact I too am aware of what the future holds.

You may still be puzzled, so allow me to share this anecdote. Two best friends Mary and Susie were walking together. Upset, Mary began talking of her birthday plans, since it seemed everyone had forgotten it. But Susie began to get agitated because she knew she had a surprise party for Mary's birthday and knew that if Mary continued to make plans herself she would ruin all of Susie's prearranged plans. So Susie knew somehow she had to let Mary know about what she had planned without giving the whole thing away. So Susie began to give her friend hints.

Well, my friend, this scenario holds true in our own lives. The times we find ourselves discouraged, confused, ready to give up, God gives a hint of what is to come to serve as reassurance. He will give you what I like to call a sneak preview. If you still do not believe me, let us take a look at people in the bible who God gave a sneak preview to.

Jeremiah, who was just a child, was given a sneak preview. In Jeremiah chapter one verse five God reveals to Jeremiah that "Before I formed you in the womb I knew you, before you were born I set you apart; I appointed you as a prophet to the nations." And that is what he became.

The exiled people in Babylon were also given a sneak preview. For Jeremiah twenty-nine verse ten through thirteen states "..."When seventy years are completed for Babylon, I will come to you and fulfill my gracious promise to bring you back to this place, For I know the plans I have for you," declares the Lord, "plans to prosper you and not to harm you, plans to give you hope and a future. Then you will call upon me and come and pray to me, and I will listen to you. You will seek me and find me when you seek me with all your heart." Wow, what encouraging news for an exiled people; to know God had already planned their escape and had already planned to give them a future that far exceeded their past.

Lastly, Joseph was given a sneak preview. In Genesis chapter thirty- seven, Joseph receives a series of dreams, revealing that he would one day rule the land. This sneak preview is what kept Joseph from giving up when his brothers sold him into slavery and when he was made one of Potiphar's prisoners. And we see in Genesis chapter forty-one verse forty-one, that Joseph's dreams became reality when Pharaoh puts him in charge of the whole land of Egypt.

But the greatest sneak preview is the one found in Revelations twenty-one and twenty-two. Here we find the sneak preview of heaven; the place where as stated in chapter twenty-one verse four "He will wipe every tear from their eyes. There will be no more death or mourning or crying or pain, for the old order of things has passed away" My God, what a place!

So whenever you get discouraged, depressed, or want to give up, think of the personal sneak preview God has given you or the sneak preview of the place with the pearly gates and streets of gold that God has waiting for us. Allow this to be your encouragement and inspiration when times get hard. A better day is coming, God's word will not return to Him void. And you will see one day your sneak preview will become the whole motion picture presentation open for the world to come and see!

Living it Up

Living Life to the Fullest

"The thief comes only to steal and kill and destroy; I have come that they may have life, and have it to the full."

-John 10:10

Broken to Be a Blessing to the World
Luke 24: 13-16; 30-31

God knew me before I was born. He created me exactly how He wanted me to be. He conducted a plan for me, all before I was conceived. But once I was conceived and birthed into this world, I was introduced to sin. Sin that separated me from God, sin that made me go my own way, sin that allowed the devil to use me, instead of God. But one day I decided it was time to give my life to God, fully and completely. But honestly the idea of God taking me and breaking me, did not appeal to me. I had been broken before. I had been broken by friends, guys, teachers, and coworkers. I did not want to relive that again; the pain, the hurt, the trying to put myself back together. You can only guess my relief when I found out that when God breaks you it is a lot different than when man does. First off when God breaks you, He has to take you in His hands... Wow what better place to be than in the hands of God. Just like a basketball in my hands will get you an airball, but a ball in Shaq's hands will win you a championship; a paintbrush in my hand you may get a rainbow, but in Picasso's hand you got million dollar art; a tennis racket in my hand may get you one hit, but in Venus Williams hands will win the Wimbledon. Well my life in my hands is reckless but in the hands of My Creator and Father... when the creation gets in the hand of the creator... just stop and imagine for a second, then give God praise. Also, it is in God's hands that you develop that intimate relationship with Him. Let's go there for a minute. You know when you are in "o boy" arms or locking hands with "o girl"; you consider that intimacy. The same applies with God when you are in His hands; you have the opportunity to get intimate with Him. That is good news when you realize that intimacy is "in to me you see". And when you begin to see into God and see into His Will for your life and His plans for your future, the joy and peace that follows surpasses all understanding.

Another reason I was slightly skeptical about the whole "breaking" concept was, I was comfortable being whole and together. Even though I had many flaws and was nowhere near my potential, I was comfortable. God had made me whole and put my broken pieces together and so I was straight... You know how you do... "God I'm good now, You made me better, so I'll just go on my way"; some are bold enough to say "God, leave me alone". But what we fail to realize is that if God was able to fix us and make us whole when we went against His will and man broke us, surely when He breaks us He can put us back together.

Lastly, it is not until you allow God to bless you and break you that you can be a blessing to others. It was not until Jesus was broken on the cross that He was able to save mankind. In Luke 24, it was not until Jesus blessed and broke the bread that the eyes of the men were opened. They were blind to who Jesus was, just like so many people today. Will you allow God to break you so their eyes can be opened? Just like when Jesus broke the two fish and five loaves of bread and blessed more than 5,000 people... you too can be a blessing at that magnitude and greater. Just allow Him to break you! Give Him what you have and present yourself to Him as a living sacrifice. Sacrifice meaning not your will but His. Sacrifice meaning sometimes you may have to be in an uncomfortable situation so someone can be delivered from theirs, and sometimes you may have to give up things in your life so someone else can have one, and have it more abundantly. But at the same time know "In all things God works for the good of those that love him, who have been called according to his purpose" (Romans 8:28). So for real this time, are you ready to be broken to be a blessing to the world?

Carpe Diem

As I sat in my Grandmother's room last night, seeing her despondent, I wanted to make her eyes open... make her hear me say I love you for the last time. As I sat listening to her breath as if each breath was her last, I wanted to just cry. But who would I be crying for... not her... she had lived a full life. She was a daughter, a sister, a wife, a mother, a grandmother, a great grandmother, an aunt, a great aunt, a friend, a neighborhood mom, a deaconess, a missionary, and so much more. She did so much and touched so many lives in her 88 years here. It was time for her to receive her reward and rest. I like to think my grandmother died empty... which is why she inspired this food for thought.

I am sure so many of us go through each day passively. We go through routines and procedures; doing just enough to get through and to get by. But I am convinced that God does not make each day, put breath in my body, give me the activity of my limbs, and show me new mercies, just for me to slack and do just enough to get me to the next day; my God is too big. There has to be more to life than going through the motions. My God is too creative, spontaneous, and expansive for me to be stuck in boxes; stuck in routines... wake up, get dressed, eat the same bagel, go the same route to school/work, walk down the same hall, say hi to the same people, wait until the same time, go home (the same route), grab a bite at the same place (same meal), go home... and so on and so forth. I want so much more. I want something fresh and something different. That is where "Carpe Diem" (Seize the Day) comes in.

Many of us wake up each morning expecting things to happen to us, instead of us taking the initiative to make things happen for ourselves. By definition seize means to grasp by force, to capture, to grab. It does not mean sit around and let each day come to you and pass you. You must take initiative. You must take every opportunity, grab every moment, and live in every second. The way I look at each and every day, is like this: Each day is a day that the Lord has made and everything He makes is good. So in spite of how I feel and in spite of situations that arise; each day is still full of life, opportunities, hope, and lessons that I have to seiz; because chances are they will not be there tomorrow. Some events and opportunities are made only for a specific day and moment. So with that mindset I enter every day, trying to squeeze every ounce of "juice" out of it, trying to exhaust it, to obtain all God placed in it for me. See achieving your full potential, doing all you were created to do, fulfilling your destiny and dying empty, are not one time events or something that happens before you die or something you will start later. They are everyday occurrences. Every day you should strive to be all you can be. Each day live life without regrets and limits! Take risk! Step out on faith! Do something spontaneous and wild! Dare to be different! Dare to be who God preordained you to be!

But not only should you get out of the box and out of "just going through the motions" routines because it hinders you living to your full potential; but also you are not the only person who knows your routines. The enemy knows your routines as well. He is watching you like a hawk and when we place ourselves in boxes and between walls it makes it so much easier for him to get to us and so much harder for us to escape. When we find ourselves caught in pointless routines, the devil does not even have to think to catch us. "It is 12 pm, I know exactly where she will be, what she will be doing and even what she will be thinking about"...

Now with all of that said... "CARPE DIEM"!!! Seize each moment of life... do not let it pass you by!!! Life is so precious and so short. Make the most of it!!! Do not live in fear! Do not live by sight! Do not hold back! Allow everything God placed in you, to be birthed.... DON'T DIE WITH LIFE IN YOU!!!

TOMORROW ISN'T PROMISED

We hear it all the time... "Tomorrow isn't promised". Growing up hearing that I always thought it was a way for people to get others to do what they wanted, when they wanted them to. Surely only sick, old, and bad people died. But as I entered high school I began to see just how wrong I was. Of course it was not until this year after the VA Tech massacre and one of my friends and her family being killed in a car crash before I really internalized that there is only one qualification for death and that is God's appointed date. The day your destiny and purpose is fulfilled is the day you are no longer needed on earth. And since none of us know when our last day is, it is so important to live each day as if it is our last and when dealing with others this is extremely important. If we treated each person as if they would be gone tomorrow, I'm convinced, grudges would diminish, forgiveness would prevail, and the petty things would be overlooked. Hatred would be at an all time low, pride would not govern our every move, and love would flourish the land just as God intended. I have said it before: there is no time to waste. Each and every day strive for excellence. Mediocrity is NOT AN OPTION! We do not serve a mediocre God; God did not give us mediocre power, so we have the responsibility to not live a life that gives God minimal glory!!! Live each and every moment as if God is standing right beside you because in all reality He is and live each moment as it may be your last cause in all reality you do not know. Oddly enough, I have found a lot of strength in watching the Saint Jude Hospital paid programs. At first I would just sit and cry when they would show a story about a child and at the end would say they died. But when I would look back at their story and some things they said in their last days about death and sickness my tears turned into tears of joy. The child knew because of what they were faced with that tomorrow was surely not promised but they did not call it quits, they did not sit around and mope... they made the most of the time they had left. They strived to make a difference and touch lives even though they knew theirs would be coming to an end. They taught me that life is truly about quality not quantity. These young kids had achieved in their short lives what it takes some people 50 years to accomplish; because they gave life their all. They lived each day as if another was not promised to them. They understood the importance of the time they were given on earth. ... So what is stopping you from achieving your full potential? What is stopping you from mending the broken relationships in your life? What is stopping you from reaching goals? What is stopping you from doing what you have always wanted to do? What is stopping you from telling that person how you feel? What is stopping you from answering God's call? What is stopping you? Just remember you do not have tomorrow... it is not promised... YOU ONLY HAVE TODAY!!!!

Jehovah Jireh
I Worship You

"God is spirit, and his worshippers must worship in spirit and in truth."

-John 4: 24

A Worship Experience

I lay prostrate before you Lord...

(My lowest posture, because I am nothing but a speck of dust

compared to you)

My face to floor....

(Showing my reverence and humility)

I begin to think of your vast greatness:

Starting with Creation and ending with my last breath.

And I become so overwhelmed with love and gratitude.

("The cross you did that just for me")

Chills run through every inch of my body and I begin to shake.

I open my mouth to speak your praises-

But that's not enough!

I have to do more!

("Words don't convey what my heart want to say")

So I begin to cry;

("God hears you through your tears")

And my mouth opens again.

But the words are not understandable to my ears;

However my spirit responds and the shaking becomes more

intense.

I feel your presence God!

I feel you holding me!

Your peace flows like a river through every inch of my body.

And I hear you tell me to talk to you... Let it all out!-

Tell Me everything you want Me to do in your life!

Become transparent!

Expose your heart! ...

And as eager as I am to have this conversation with You Daddy;

When I open my mouth to speak it's not me talking at all.

It can't be!-

I've never spoke with such authority and confidence!

I've never claimed things so far out of my reach!

I've never acknowledged or accepted visions that seem so surreal!

I've never been so ready, God!

I've never been so open to your move!

I've never had such a strong desire to be close to you!

In this moment of exposure I feel my spiritual being, being elevated to that next level.

I feel all fear being diminished!

My purpose is redefined!

I see nothing but victory and success!

Visions and dreams are revived!

It's too much to contain -

My cup runneth over!

All I can do is lay prostrate on my face and bathe in Your presence.

Lord, You Are...

I worship You for who You are.

You are the bright and morning star.

You are my Redeemer and my Friend.

The Author and Finisher of my end.

You are my joy and my laughter.

To be more like you is what I am after.

You are my peace right in my storm.

You take my crazy life and return it to norm.

You restore me when I'm weary at heart.

You wake me up everyday with a brand new start...

Lord, I could go on for days,

Because you are so magnificent in all your ways.

You are my Savior; my Christ,

Your grace, it will always suffice.

You've never left me and never will...

You said to the winds and waves to just be still.

You healed the lame, deaf, and blind.

You turned water into wine.

You worked many miracles during Your day,

And You had such an awesome price to pay.

You sacrificed Your life so that I would be free;

YOU GAVE YOUR LIFE JUST FOR ME!!!

Jesus, just to call your name,

Takes away the pain and all of the shame.

Nothing else matters when I think of You; of who You are,

My Prince of Peace, my bright and morning Star!

The only one who comes to see about me every time I call-

You are my everything; You are MY ALL!!!

LOVE

We had not had the pleasure of meeting yet, but You knew all about me; everything there was to know about me. Not only the good things that I am quick to rattle off during an interview or in front of company; but You knew the things I am still in denial and repulse about. Even still, You did not let that change how You felt about me. If anything it was those unmentionable things that made You love me more, because in my weakness You saw Your strength. There was really nothing I could do to make You love me any less. But You realized my sin would push us apart. You saw that my faults would make it impossible for us to bond. Then one day, the thought of us not having a relationship and not spending eternity together began to sadden You. The thought of me spending forever in eternal damnation broke Your heart. So you decided to do something about it; and this part blows my mind each and every time. You took on my form through Your Son. You came off of Your throne to walk the place that I would have to walk 2000 years later. You came here to overcome and defeat every problem that I would ever face in life, so I would not only have a powerful God but an understanding God; a God who could relate. You love me so much that You want to feel my pain with me. But Your love did not stop there. You gave Your Son's life as a ransom for mine; just so I could enjoy an abundant, everlasting life in sweet communion with You. And not only was Your Son 100% man like me, He was 100% You... That's just like You, always demonstrating and never asking me to do something You wouldn't do Yourself. You came as the example of the life You want me to lead. Even more, You ask me to die daily to my flesh because one day you too had to die to Yours. And then one day we met. I remember it like it was yesterday... You told me about Your sacrifice and why You did it and I began to cry and thank You for the love You had for me and You corrected me and said "have". You let me know that Your love could now be completed in me and now that the feeling was reciprocated it made You happy. Wow, we had just met, I hadn't even learned how to please You yet and already I had made You smile. And as

I have continued through life Your love has become a driving force in me; after all it is Your driving force. Your love causes You to save and deliver. Your love is the reason You daily extend grace, mercy, and compassion to me. Your love is seen in Your forgiveness. Your love is evident to me every morning I wake up with breath in my body. Even those times I do things that are not pleasing to You, Your unconditional love is still there. Those times when I do things to hurt myself, Your love comforts me. In dark times Your love is my light; it is my hope, my joy, and my peace. Those days where I can't find a single soul to care... Your love encompasses me; and I feel that even if I had the love of every person on Earth it still couldn't compare. Those days I feel like I can't go on and all I can do is cry Your love meets me right where I am and holds me until the tears cease. And those days I feel I am on top of the world Your love takes me even higher. Surely, Whitney Houston was mistaken when she said the greatest love of all was learning to love yourself, because it wasn't until I learned to love You that I even thought about loving myself. I couldn't even smile in the mirror until I found out that You loved me so much that even before the foundations of the Earth You ordered my steps and planned out my destiny. Your love for me is forever, which doesn't just mean it will be now into eternity but it stretches infinitely both ways. My mind cannot even grasp the full concept of Your love, but I know it fills me; and I know I want to demonstrate the love You have for me. I want to love people past what they've done to me. I want to love people for their potential, for who You are molding them to be. I want to love people in spite of our disagreements, pride, and egos. I want to love with pure love. Love not based on how a person treats me or the wrong they have done but on the fact that they are one of Your precious creations and You love them. I don't want to love for corrupt motives or for personal gain. I want to love because You commanded me to love, it pleases You, and it frees me. So even now as Your love floods and overwhelms me I thank You for it. But moreover I thank You for loving me before I knew You.

Psalm 23

Going to a Christian school, being brought up in a Christian home, going to Sunday School and Vacation Bible School; there were just certain things that you were supposed to know. Everybody was supposed to know that Eve ate the apple, Cain killed Abel, Jacob stole Esau's birthright, Joshua fought the battle of Jericho, David slayed Goliath, Noah built an Ark, Moses parted the Red Sea, Jonah got swallowed by a whale, Joseph had a colorful coat, and Daniel was stuck in a lion's den. Everybody knew there were 66 books of the bible; 39 in the Old Testament, 27 in the New Testament. Everyone knew father Abraham had many sons, the B-I-B-L-E was the book for "me" and that there was a fountain flowing "Deep and Wide". Everyone knew that "the Word of God is a lamp unto my feet...", "I can do all things...", "For God so loved the world...", "Make a joyful noise unto the Lord..." and "The Lord is my Shepherd...". But it was not until I got older and I started applying these stories and scriptures to my everyday life and situations that any of it became effective. It was not until I started personalizing the scriptures and stories that they became of any use to me... And that is what I did with the 23rd Psalm. Growing up it was something we were taught to rattle off when asked, and it really was not a scripture you thought about. But lately I have found myself reading it over and over and reciting it before I leave the house and before I go to sleep and finding so much comfort and strength in it. So I figured how much more meaningful and powerful it would be for me, if I was to put it in my own words. Well here goes...

Lord, you are my leader.
You guide me,
And You watch over me.
Everything I need and want,
You readily provide.
If it is in Your will,
Its just a prayer away.
When chaos and stress engulf me;
You lead me to that place-
That place of peace and tranquility.
It's there that You give me rest.

You give me peace.

You restore me.

Lord, You order my steps.

Lord, You teach me Your ways,

All to bring glory to Your name.

And as I deal with the devils attacks,

And I constantly encounter his traps,

I'm not afraid.

Your protection brings me comfort.

You bless me and show me favor,

In front of people who hate me-

The people who want to see me fail;

You elevate me right before their eyes.

Your precious anointing and blessings

Flow abundantly in my life.

Lord, Your grace and mercy,

Your love and joy,

Your peace and power,

Will be with me for the rest of my life.

And I will forever stay in Your presence.

Lord, Prepare Me...

To Be a Sanctuary

"Create in me a pure heart, O God, and
renew a steadfast spirit within me."
Psalm 51:10

20/20 Vision

With each person I see;
I no longer see their faults, but their good.
I don't see their past failures,
but their goals.
I don't see what they use to be,
but what they are going to be.

With every bad situation;
I don't see the bad beginning but the victorious end.
I don't see the obstacles,
but the great accomplishment.
I don't see the bind,
but the awesome deliverance.

With every challenge, I see opportunity!
With every mistake, I see change!
With every confrontation, I see resolution!
With every negative, I see a positive!
And with every little thing, I see a God who's bigger.

We have all heard the saying, "I have to see it to believe it". And some may say that this defies what faith is all about; but I don't believe it does, because vision is not just in the physical world, but you can see things both mentally and spiritually. Even though we have never seen God or the air, each of us has a mental picture, thought, or idea that we associate with them. Seeing is truly believing. Not only is life based on the things you see, it is based on how these sights are perceived. For example, whether you see the glass half empty or half full determines how fast you drink what is inside. Many people underestimate how much their outlook on life can affect every aspect of their life. But can you just imagine for a second the quality of life you would have if you began to envision things in a positive, more Godly light. Many of us know the power of the tongue and the ability of it to speak life or death over a situation. But there is also power in the "eyes" and how you see a situation. So the challenge is to begin to see the good in EVERYTHING, even if it is just a little or even if you have to dig deep to find it.

A Finished Chapter

I'm running out of pages;
This chapter is soon to end.
I knew one day it was coming;
I just didn't know when.

But now I know its time.
I can finally stand on my own.
A tree is finally starting to grow,
From the seeds that have been sown.

I've finally organized and taken in
All that has been said to me.
Some things didn't make sense at first;
But now those things I clearly see.

No longer am I scared of the day-
The day I will have to be my own person.
But now I am convinced, it is not scary,
Surely it is a task that can be done.

I've learned so much from my mistakes,
And I know definitely not to make them again.
Because my future and where I'm going

It's so much better than where I been.

So its time for a fresh start,
And its time for a new me.
Its time to say bye to the hurt,
And hi to the new Jocelyn healed totally.

Yes, me with a new heart, mind, and soul
A heart, no longer broken with cracks.
A mind, renewed and focused.
And a soul that's complete and no longer lacks.

This is how I am going to enter my next chapter.
But for now...

Wow, I made it to the end of this chapter.
One chapter down in this book of life.
Wow I made it to the end of this chapter.
A chapter filled with its fair share of pain and strife.

Some days I didn't think I would make it,
But I survived.
Some days I wanted to give up...
But I strived.

And I'm glad I did,

Because look at me now.

I made it!

And I don't have to ask how.

It was nobody but God!

He's given me all I need.

And for the rest of my life

I'll always follow His lead.

Because after all, He's already wrote my book;

He knows the beginning and the end.

And I couldn't think of a better person to write it,

Since He is my dearest and closest friend.

112

Baking (Tried in the Fire)

I saw a baker take a handful of dough in his hand,
And looking at the dough he thought of all it could be.
But right then I didn't fully understand;
Then I began to think of the dough as me....

And as the baker kneaded and pounded the dough,
And took a rolling pin and flattened it out;
The relevance of what I saw began to grow.
I already knew what this lesson was about.

Finally the baker had molded the dough just right,
Adding to this loaf specific ingredients he wanted it to possess.
He then began to marvel at it in delight,
Thinking of all the people this food would bless.

But he knew it wasn't quite ready yet;
The yeast placed inside had to rise.
He knew this was a step that he couldn't forget,
Or this could lead to the bread's demise.

So he sat a while, and patiently watched the dough expand.
Even though it took hours it didn't bother him one bit.

Because he knew that his creation would be grand;
He knew all his time and effort would be worth it

Finally the dough had risen how it should,
And it was time to put it in the heat.
The baker knew he had done all he could.
Now in the oven, this process had to complete.

But he did not leave the bread's side as it cooked.
No, he sat beside the stove the whole time.
And inside the stove, every now and then, he looked,
Waiting for the bread to reach its prime.

Making sure the bread browned just perfectly,
Making sure the bread didn't burn at all.
Making sure the bread baked correctly,
Making sure the bread didn't fall.

The baker sat there only an arm lengths away,
To make sure nothing happened to his creation.
The baker sat there to make sure everything was okay,
Waiting for the product of all his preparation.

But I couldn't help thinking of all the bread had to go through;

Then all of a sudden from the oven came a wonderful smell.

And all of the things the bread had to endure and do

Seemed necessary for it end up well,

Because when the bread emerged from the oven, it was done.

No longer was it many ingredients, useless and raw.

No, they had been merged and baked into one,

And the end product had me stunned in awe.

The end product was a loaf that the baker was so proud of;

A loaf of bread he placed in a package that could carry it around,

Because this loaf of bread brought the baker so much love

He wanted it to be spread from person to person all over the

town.

And that was possible now that the baking process was complete.

Yes, now the lump of dough was ready for everyone to share and

eat!

One day I saw a baker take a handful of dough in his hand,

And looking at the dough he thought of all it could be...

Right then and there I didn't fully understand,

But now I know the Baker is God and the piece of dough is Me!!!

Changes

Imagine me! Imagine me! ...

I don't have to imagine no more,

Cause I've walked through a whole new door!

My faith has taken a drastic increase.

And my prayers, they never seem to cease.

Your glory has become evident to me,

And your plan for my life I'm beginning to see.

I've climbed to new heights

And developed such insight,

That I don't know how I ever lived without you.

God you made my life so new!

You've changed my walk!

You've changed my talk!

You saved me from the pits of hell!

You gave me such a story to tell!

You've anointed my hands,

And given me holy boldness to take a stand!

Your grace and mercy have given me a new start!

You came in and changed the desires of my heart!

You redirected my path and my way-

I'm so glad these changes are here to stay!

I WANT IT ALL

God I know you have so much more for me.

There's so much more you want me to be;

So much more to this Manifest Destiny.

More to this vision, that I can't see.

Heights that I can't reach till I trust totally,

Serve you faithfully,

Love you wholeheartedly,

Commit myself completely ...

But no matter what I have to do

To get to that place in you.

I'm going to give it my all.

I'm going to continue to follow your call.

Because I want all you have for me,

And to be all that I can be.

Girl Talk

Inspired By Many Tragedies

"They overcame him by the blood of the
Lamb and by the word of their
testimony"
-Revelations 12:11

I SPEAK LIFE

(Dedicated to every girl who has ever had an abortion)

I speak life-

No;

I took life.

I had the chance to birth the next Maya Angelou, Malcolm X or

Dr. King;

But instead I thought of my baby as a thing.

A thing, a burden, a hassle-

I traded motherhood for a tassel.

True, I'm only sixteen-

But there is a million people who would have been

happy to have my great bundle of joy;

who would have showered her with love, money, and toys.

But I didn't give her the chances I had-

...And now that I think about it, I'm kind of glad.

Did I want her to have to deal with what I did?

Have all the secrets and pain that I hid?

Find love and pleasure in boys and men?

Pile sin upon sin upon sin upon sin?

Live in a world of lust, sex, and lies?

Every night lie in bed and muffle her cries?

Feel only worth something when she's on her knees or back?

Want to die because of all the qualities she lacks?

Everyday getting raped, beat, and cursed?

Holding in all the pain; feeling as if she will burst?

Popping pill after pill; making cut after cut.

Trying hard to escape the life of a slut-

Body polluted from all the spirits and STDs.

Trying to lock down but everyone got keys.

Trying harder to hold on to a piece of herself...

No, I can't let my baby go through all I did!

When the time is right I want her to enjoy being a kid.

I want her to find love and pleasure in what is pure.

I want her not to contract AIDS but find a cure.

I want her to know she is the most beautiful of God's creatures.

And her brain is her best and most valuable feature.

I never want her to shed a tear,

Or be consumed by any fear.

I want her to dream,

and not accept life the way it seems.

I never want her to be robbed of her virginity.

I want her to live on for eternity;

Not to die and burn in hell,

But to go to heaven where all is well.

But now more than ever before-

I don't want my baby to be a bastard and her mother a whore!

The Greatest Love on Earth (Mirror)

(Dedicated to every girl who has struggled with low self esteem)

I saw a girl staring directly in my eyes;

So I decided to stare directly back into hers.

And what I saw saddened my heart,

Because in her eyes I saw the deepest pain.

I saw the greatest fear and the worse loneliness.

But as I continued to stare in her eyes;

I saw past the hurt at her surface,

And I saw the strength and joy deep inside.

I saw past her confusion and saw peace in her soul.

I saw past her frustration, her anger, her shackles,

And I saw a girl free without a care in this world...

I couldn't help but smile at what I saw,

And I noticed she was smiling back at me.

Maybe she could see what I saw too-

But maybe she couldn't.

Maybe she couldn't see her beauty and greatness.

Maybe she couldn't see her potential and shine...

I felt my eyes fill with tears as I watched hers do the same.

I began to freely cry as tear after tear fell from her eyes.

How could such a beautiful creation cry such ugly tears?

I imagined each one of her tears carrying one of her troubles;

Each tear carrying her pain;

Falling to the ground,

Shattering,

Freeing her...

And as this process cleansed her,

I began to see her true form; her pure form.

And instantly I began to love her.

I loved everything about her.

I praised the God that made her.

And I knew I had found a friend for life.

But as I turned around and walked away, she didn't follow.

I looked back to see her standing there looking directly at me.

And that's when reality hit....

I HAD BEEN LOOKING IN A MIRROR AND HAD BEGUN TO LOVE MYSELF!!!

They Told Me

(Dedicated to every girl who has ever been a people pleaser)

They told me to let my hair grow.
Even though I liked it short,
I asked "How long?"

They told me to cut my nails.
Even though I liked them long,
I asked "How short?"

They told me to stop wearing that color.
Even though it was my favorite,
I stopped.

They told me not to watch that show.
Even though it was my favorite,
I turned it off.

They told me not to eat that food.
Even though it was my comfort,
I gave it up.

They told me not to talk to her.
Even though she was my best friend,
I said good bye.

They told me not to talk to him.
Even though he was my boo,
I broke it off.

They told me I ought to be happy.
Even though I was sad,
I smiled.

They told me I ought to be sad.
Even though I was happy,
I cried.

They told me exactly what they thought about me.
Even though I hid my true feelings about them
I lied.

They said it was constructive.
Even though I thought it was cruel,
I accepted.

They told me what not to do.
Even though they did it,
I ignored it.

They told me all my wrongs.
Even though I saw most of theirs,
I dismissed them.

They told me they would always be there.
Even though they weren't,
I pretended they were.

They told me they loved me.
Even though it rarely showed,
I believed them.

...

Then one day they told me to just be myself.
Even though it should have been easy,
I asked them "How?"

They told me, "by not seeking out any approval".
Even though the only one i sought out was theirs,
I said ok.

They told me, "by not stressing over what others thought".
Even though I only cared what they thought,
I said that's fine.

They told me, "by not letting others define me".

Even though I had only used their definitions,

I said alright.

They told me, "by not getting upset when others don't agree with my decisions"...

Even though I'm sure they didn't agree with my next decision....

I had decided THEY HAD TOLD ME ENOUGH!!!!!

TO MY LADIES:

Hey sistas! When will we learn,

Our virginity is not a giveaway its got to be earned?

But not by just any random man-

But the one God sends to put a ring on your hand!

I'm so tired of sex being looked at like a hobby-

"Meet me this weekend in the hotel lobby".

If you ain't doing it, you ain't cool.

We got STDs running rampant in the school

To my beautiful young royal queens:

You don't really know if he is truly clean.

He could be lying just to get inside those jeans-

Come on ladies STOP BEING NAÏVE!

Stop acting like AIDS can't happen to you-

Yes you can get pregnant your first time too!

Those booty calls, those one night stands-

Hopping from bed to bed and from man to man.

It may not seem to affect you now,

But it's going to catch up with you someway, somehow.

You can't continue to live in sin,

And expect a happily ever after end.

Sooner or later, it's going to blow up in your face-

But you can change now: you're not a hopeless case!!!

God wants to purify you and make you whole,

You're not too young and you're not too old!

No matter how long you been going this way-

God is saying tomorrow is a brand new day!

You can walk away from the guilt and shame!

Let God restore your spirit and clear your name.

Become dependent on HIM and not on man;

Because He can give you far more pleasure than that boy can!

Late in the midnight hour, when you would normally be in

someone else's bed-

Know that God can now hold you instead.

HE won't ever ditch you for something new;

Or try to take advantage of you.

He just wants to be your lover and friend;

And now my plea to you has come to end.

So, now you know what you need to do-

And know I'll continue to pray for you!

WWJD

"As I look out unto the world there's some things that I see that I wanna talk about. Can I talk about them?"- Kirk Franklin

Talk Jocelyn...

I use to always get upset when I heard someone refer to my generation as the lost generation but now I'm beginning to think... There are so many things I see that are hurting and upsetting me... and I'm not trying to be judgmental because we have all fallen short of the glory of God and I stand guilty of many of these things. But anyway, we have taken disrespect to a whole new level. We disrespect ourselves, each other, our parents, and other adults in our lives and it has become accepted and I am tired of it. We spend more time tearing each other down than building each other up. We spend more time hating on someone and their gifts and talents and less figuring out how we can benefit from them. We now have beautiful females acting and dressing much older than what they are, playing grown up games and act like the world is coming to an end when they are faced with the grown up consequences. I am tired of young men with bright and promising futures throwing them away to imitate images seen on TV; when in reality they know that is not who they are. I am tired of sex being accepted… being something to brag about, being a defining factor. The titles placed before names everyday by our peers is based strictly on sex. There are playas and pimps, jump offs, teases, bobble heads, slut buckets, whores… you all know. It seems no one has a mind of their own anymore. Everyone is striving to be like everyone else, instead of striving to be like Jesus. There seems to be less original lingo, style, thoughts and ideas. No one is willing to take a stand anymore. We see someone getting joked we laugh and jump in, a fight breaks out and we get our hits in. But when will these immaturities stop attracting us? When will our need to be accepted and part of a bigger cause lead us to organizations like the bible club, church choir, or class council, instead of violent self destructive gangs? When will our need for money be solved by legitimacy? Come on, when are we going to get a clue? Beautiful queens, when will we see that once is a mistake, twice is a slip up, and your third time its intentional... How can we continue to kill God's creations? I believe abortions and birth control have become crutches. They give females excuses to destroy their temples and not deal with the full consequences of their actions. And I commend all the teenage mothers out there for not taking the easy way out, but I am convinced with all the condoms and birth control out there, even though they are crutches, I should not have just counted six unborn babies walking down one school hall. Oh, but there is more... God made Adam and Eve not Adam and Steve. Homo and bi sexuality has become the norm. Am I the only one disturbed by females making out and boys holding hands? ... Ok, it's true I am disturbed by the playas and the hoes, the drug dealers, gang bangers, and baby mamas, but my biggest disgust ain't with the sex, lies, babies, and drugs. No, my biggest disgust is with "us": the "church" kids. "The saved, sanctified, holy ghost filled, fire baptized, run on see what the end going to be" kids. It is us, the lights of the world; the salt of the earth. It is us, the phony, selfish, hypocrites. We receive the gift of salvation and will not even introduce others to the Giver. We have this "I'm going to heaven anyhow" mentality and we allow our friends and others we suppose to care about to live and die in hell. We accept their sins. "Well if she like it, I love it" and it is that same love that's corrupting her life… We take the same mouth we praise God with, and cuss somebody out. We will be quick to spread gossip but not the gospel. We are quick to tell what a boy/girl has done for us but hesitant to tell of the goodness of the Lord. Have we taken the desire to be liked and accepted and put it before the desire to please God? My God, what will it take to wake us up? To shatter our comfort zone? To open our eyes to the filth we are laying in? When will the day come when people will know we are Christians by our love, our actions, and our words? … Young People we've got to take a stand!!!

www.ingramcontent.com/pod-product-compliance
Lightning Source LLC
LaVergne TN
LVHW011244080426
835509LV00005B/625